T0197255

The Newbies

Christmas Sight Words Activities and Coloring Book

Barbara D. Hendricks
and
Denise A.L. Hendricks

authorHOUSE

AuthorHouse™
1663 Liberty Drive
Bloomington, IN 47403
www.authorhouse.com
Phone: 1 (800) 839-8640

Published by AuthorHouse   12/14/2016

ISBN: 978-1-5246-4682-0 (sc)
ISBN: 978-1-5246-4681-3 (e)

About the Authors

<u>Barbara D. Hendricks</u> is a writer and the owner of Broader Horizons Childcare & Development Inc. Barbara has owned her own daycare for 23 years and counting. She wanted to create a whole new children's book series that she could read to her new grandchildren and others. When they were born, God spoke to her and told her to write a children's book series. Barbara felt as if she had a new transformed life. Barbara D. Hendricks lives in Chicago, Illinois. She is a mother of four, a grandmother of 16 and counting, a foster parent for 22 years and counting. This children's book series is important to her because it reminds her of how much she loves to teach children. In her spare time, Barbara likes to help educate families on how to restore their credit.

<u>Denise A. L. Hendricks</u> is a loving and caring mother of 3. Denise loves to help others and is a Lifetime Girl Scout of Girl Scouts of Greater Chicago and Northwest Indiana. Denise loves to travel and help her community. She spending her time with her family and children. Denise's favorite things to do is read and spend time reading with her children.

Santa Claus

Papá Noel

Snowman

el muñeco de nieve

Christmas Tree

el árbol de Navidad

Which Christmas Wreath is different?

¿cual guirnalda de la Navidad es diferente?

Decorate your own Christmas Trees

decorar tu propio árbol de Navidad

Stocking

la calceta

Bell

la campana

Lights

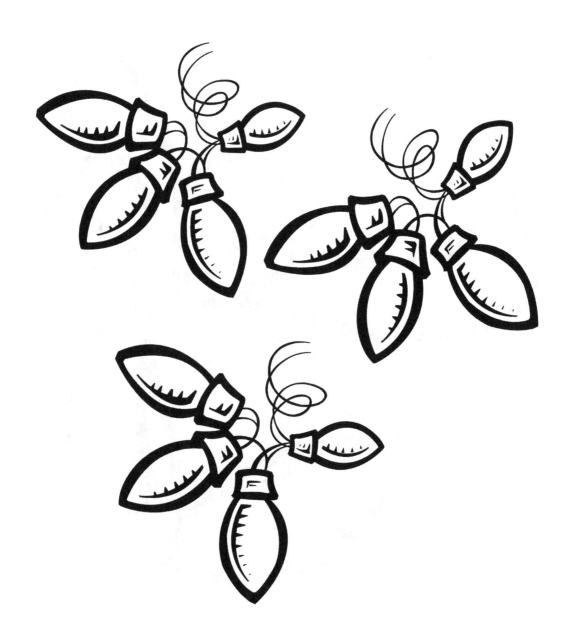

la luz

Toys

el juguete

Connect the dots to make a gift

Conectar los puntos para hacer un regalo

Ornament

ornamento

Love

Amor

Star

la estrella

Christmas Card

HOLIDAY GREETINGS

tarjeta de Navidad

Circle your favorite Christmas Foods

Círculo de sus comidas favoritas de Navidad

Mrs. Santa Claus

ropa de veraneo

Snow Globe

globo de la nieve

Christmas Movie

Película de navidad

Games

el juego

Pajamas

el piyama

Angels

el ángel

How many Reindeers do you see?

¿Cuántos renos ves?

Garland

la guirnalda

Decorate the cookies

Decorar las galletas

Rudolf the Red Nose Reindeer
What color is Rudolf's nose?

Rudolf el reno de la nariz roja
¿De qué color es la nariz de Rudolf?

Carriage

el carruaje

Snow Flakes

Copo de nieve

Winter Jacket

chaqueta de invierno

Draw a line to connect the mittens that match

**dibujar una línea para
conectar los mitones que**

Hats

el sombrero

Scarf

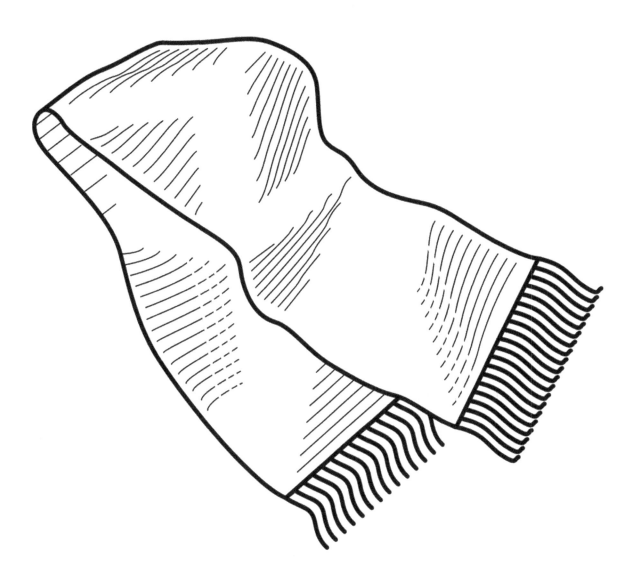

la bufanda

Family

la familia

Giving

Generoso

Christmas Songs

canciones de Navidad

Sleigh

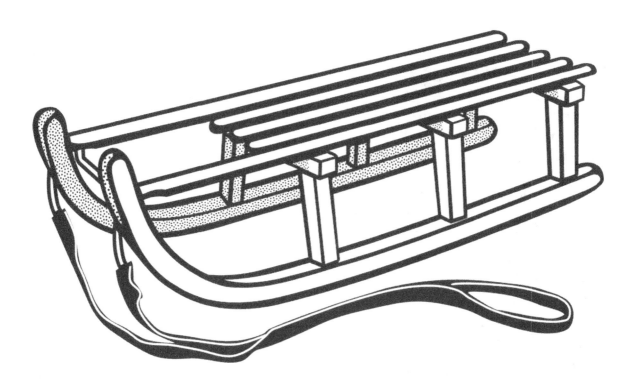

el trineo

Who is invited to your Christmas Party?

¿que se invita a su fiesta de Navidad?

Which Bow is the biggest?

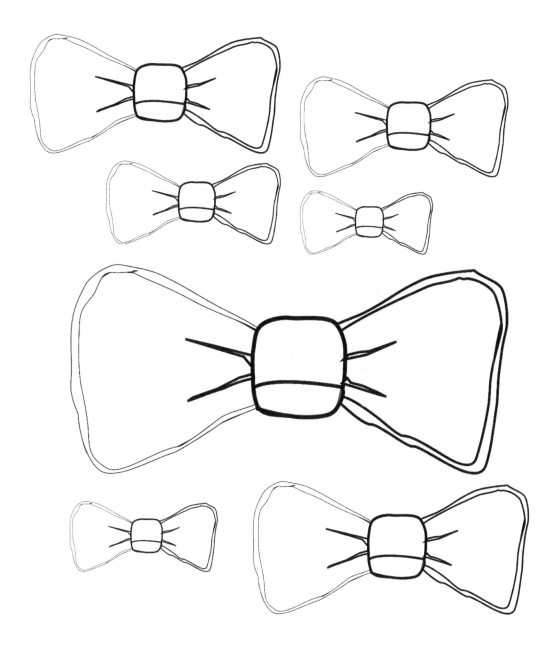

¿que el arco es más grande?

Pepperments

la menta

Connect the dots to make a Candy Cane

Conectar los puntos para hacer un Candy Cane

North Pole

Polo Norte

Christmas Town

Ciudad de Navidad

Which Christmas
Penguin is different?

¿Qué pingüino de Navidad
es diferente?

How many candles do you see?

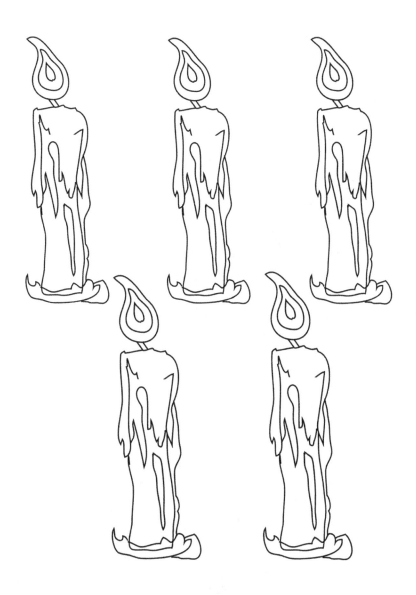

¿Cuántas velas ves?

Manger

el pesebre

Baby Jesus

Niño Jesús

Donkey

el burro

Mary

María

Joseph

José

How many Wise Men do you see?

¿Cuántos sabios ves?

Ice Skating

el patinaje

Gingerbread House

la casa de pan de jengibre

Draw a Holiday Picture

Dibujar un cuadro de vacaciones

To God Be the Glory

Other books by The Newbies:
The Newbies
Los Newbies

The Newbies Bible Alphabets A-Z
Los Newbies Alfabetos de la Biblia A-Z

The Newbies Bible Alphabets A-Z Activities and Coloring Book
Los Alfabetos de la Biblia Newbies A-Z Actividades y Libro de Colorear

Barbara D. Hendricks
Co-Author Denise A.L. Hendricks

Jay
Paris
Gabby
Gia

To Contact us at: the_newbies@yahoo.com.
Follow us on twitter @_TheNewbies,
Facebook@TheNewbies,
Instagram@_thenewbies.
Check out our website at: www.newbiesseries.com.

The Newbies Book Series
P.O.Box 63
Hazel Crest, IL 60429

Printed in the United States
By Bookmasters